To Nick and Nikki H, my lifetime beach buddies M. B.
For Eva, Iván and Olov J. V.

First published 2021
by Nosy Crow Ltd
The Crow's Nest, 14 Baden Place
Crosby Row, London SE1 1YW
www.nosycrow.com

ISBN 978 1 78800 413 8 (HB)
ISBN 978 1 83994 083 5 (PB)

'The National Trust' and the oak leaf logo are registered trademarks of The National Trust
(Enterprises) Limited (a subsidiary of The National Trust for Places of Historic Interest or
Natural Beauty, Registered Charity Number 205846).

Nosy Crow and associated logos are trademarks and/or registered trademarks of
Nosy Crow Ltd (Registered Company Number 7130282).

A CIP catalogue record for this book is available
from the British Library.

Printed in China

Papers used by Nosy Crow are made from
wood grown in sustainable forests.

10 9 8 7 6 5 4 3 2 1 (HB)
10 9 8 7 6 5 4 3 2 1 (PB)

MOIRA BUTTERFIELD JESÚS VERONA

LOOK
WHAT I FOUND
at the Seaside

nosy crow

Chasing waves and having fun,
water sparkling in the sun . . .

Look what I found!
A curly seashell. Inside it shines bright, like a pearl.

Can you also see . . . ?
One shell shaped like a little fan
Two tiny crabs on the sand
Three shells shaped like long,
curly trumpets

There are spiky shells and smooth shells, flat shells, long shells and shells that twist round and round.

A seashell is armour that an animal from the sea grows to protect itself.

Creatures such as sea snails live inside seashells. Make sure a shell is empty before you pick it up. It could be someone's house!

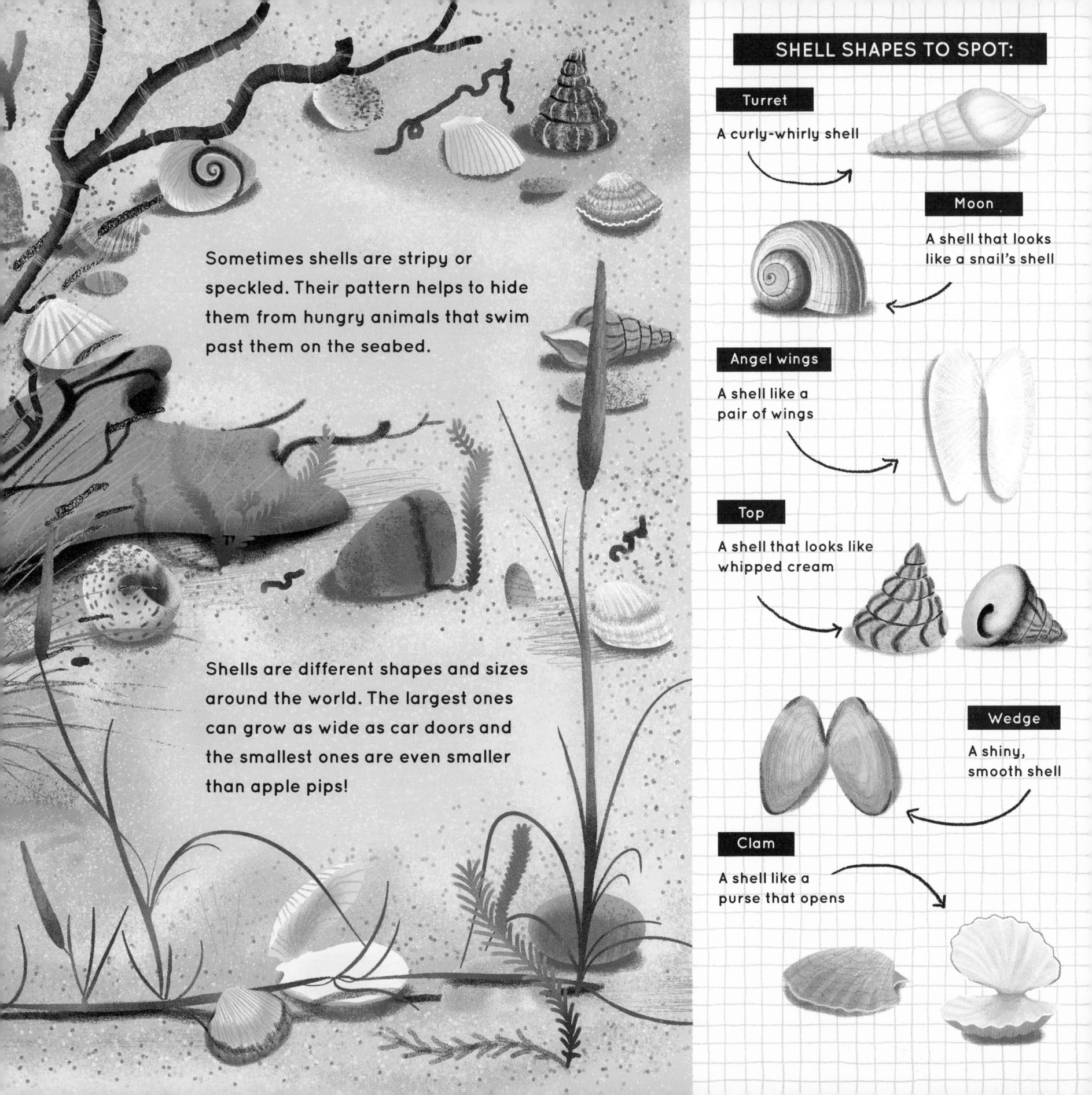

Sometimes shells are stripy or speckled. Their pattern helps to hide them from hungry animals that swim past them on the seabed.

Shells are different shapes and sizes around the world. The largest ones can grow as wide as car doors and the smallest ones are even smaller than apple pips!

SHELL SHAPES TO SPOT:

Turret

A curly-whirly shell

Moon

A shell that looks like a snail's shell

Angel wings

A shell like a pair of wings

Top

A shell that looks like whipped cream

Wedge

A shiny, smooth shell

Clam

A shell like a purse that opens

Searching rock pools with a net.
Welly boots are getting wet!

Look what I found!

A round, white pebble.
It feels smooth in my fingers.

Can you also see . . . ?
One speckly starfish
Two little fish
Three swimming shrimps

When you hold a pebble you are touching something very old. It began as rock made millions of years ago. The water has tumbled and turned the rock until it has worn smooth and small.

The stripes and spots on some pebbles are made by different types of rock or crystal squished together like layers in a sandwich.

You might find some milky blue, green or white sea glass on a beach too. It is glass that has been made smooth by the waves.

Sometimes pebbles have round holes in them. Small creatures such as sea worms have scraped the holes out to make a hiding place.

PEBBLES TO SPOT:

Quartz
A milky-coloured glittery crystal

Quartzite
Grey with red or yellow patches

Sandstone
A pebble that looks like grains of sand

Granite
Grey with dark grains in it

Serpentinite
Dark green and grey streaks

Feldspar
Orangey-pink and white

Search the seaweed, soft and curled,
from an underwater world.

Look what I found!
An empty crab shell.
It looks like a frilly pink dish.

Can you also see . . . ?
One message in a bottle
Two seagulls looking for food
Three different colours of seaweed
— red, green and brown

Sometimes crabs grow too big for their shells, just like you might grow too big for your shoes. Their old shells might get washed in by the tide.

The shell feels too tight, so the crab wriggles out from inside. It's called moulting.

A crab has a new soft shell under its old one. Once it has moulted it must hide somewhere safe underwater while its new shell hardens.

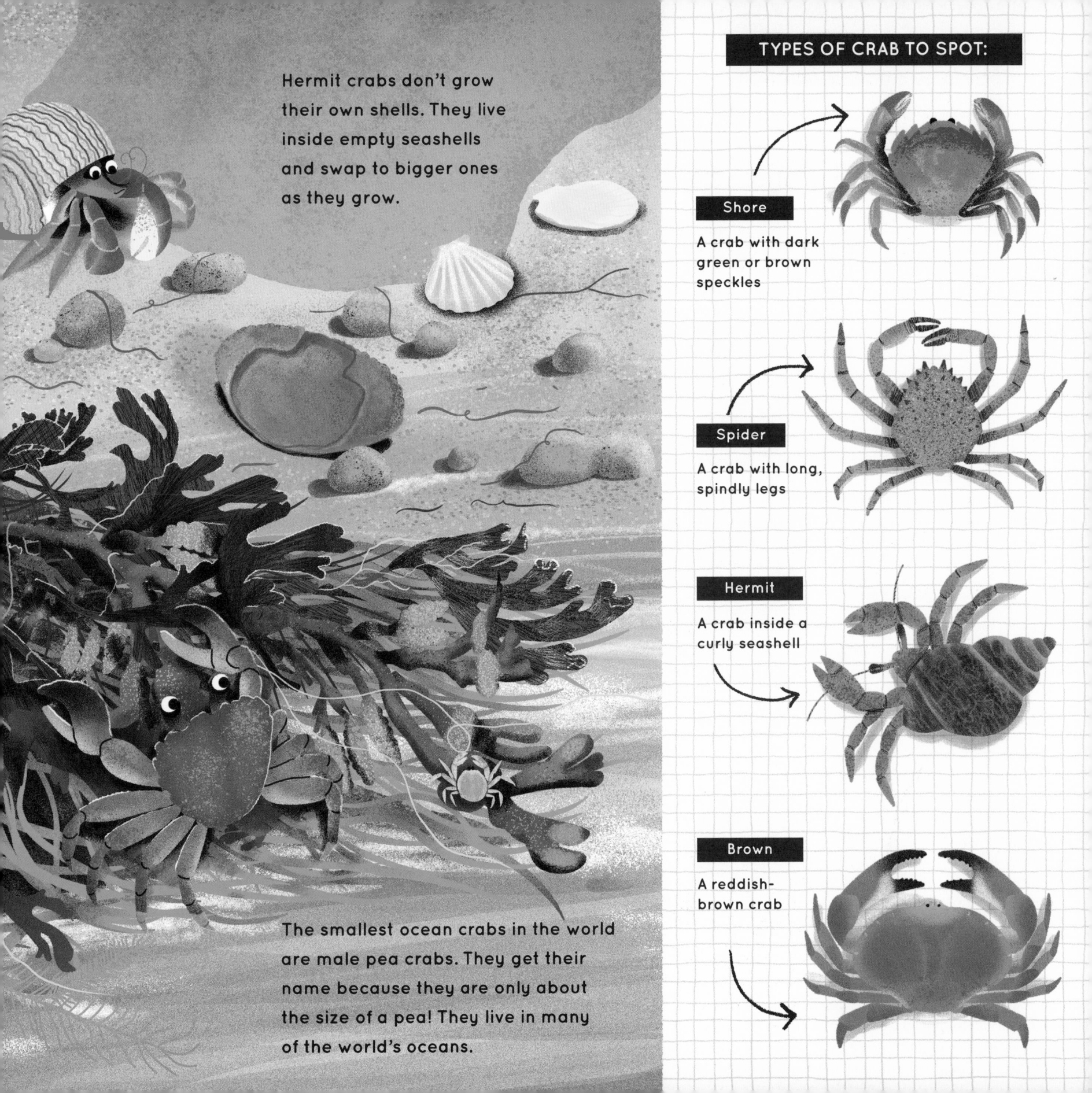

Hermit crabs don't grow their own shells. They live inside empty seashells and swap to bigger ones as they grow.

The smallest ocean crabs in the world are male pea crabs. They get their name because they are only about the size of a pea! They live in many of the world's oceans.

TYPES OF CRAB TO SPOT:

Shore

A crab with dark green or brown speckles

Spider

A crab with long, spindly legs

Hermit

A crab inside a curly seashell

Brown

A reddish-brown crab

There's a cave carved by the tide.
It's wet and dark. Let's stay outside.

Look what I found!

A mermaid's purse, with little hooks on it.
What would a mermaid keep inside it?

Can you also see . . . ?
One pile of pebbles someone
has made
Two pieces of silvery driftwood
washed in by the sea
Three limpet shells shaped like
pointy hats

A mermaid's purse doesn't really belong to a mermaid. It's an egg case for a sea creature — a small shark, a skate fish or a ray.

The egg case has hooks that anchor it to rocks or seaweed underwater, while the baby fish grows safely inside.

When the fish is ready to leave, it wriggles out of one end like money sliding out of a purse.

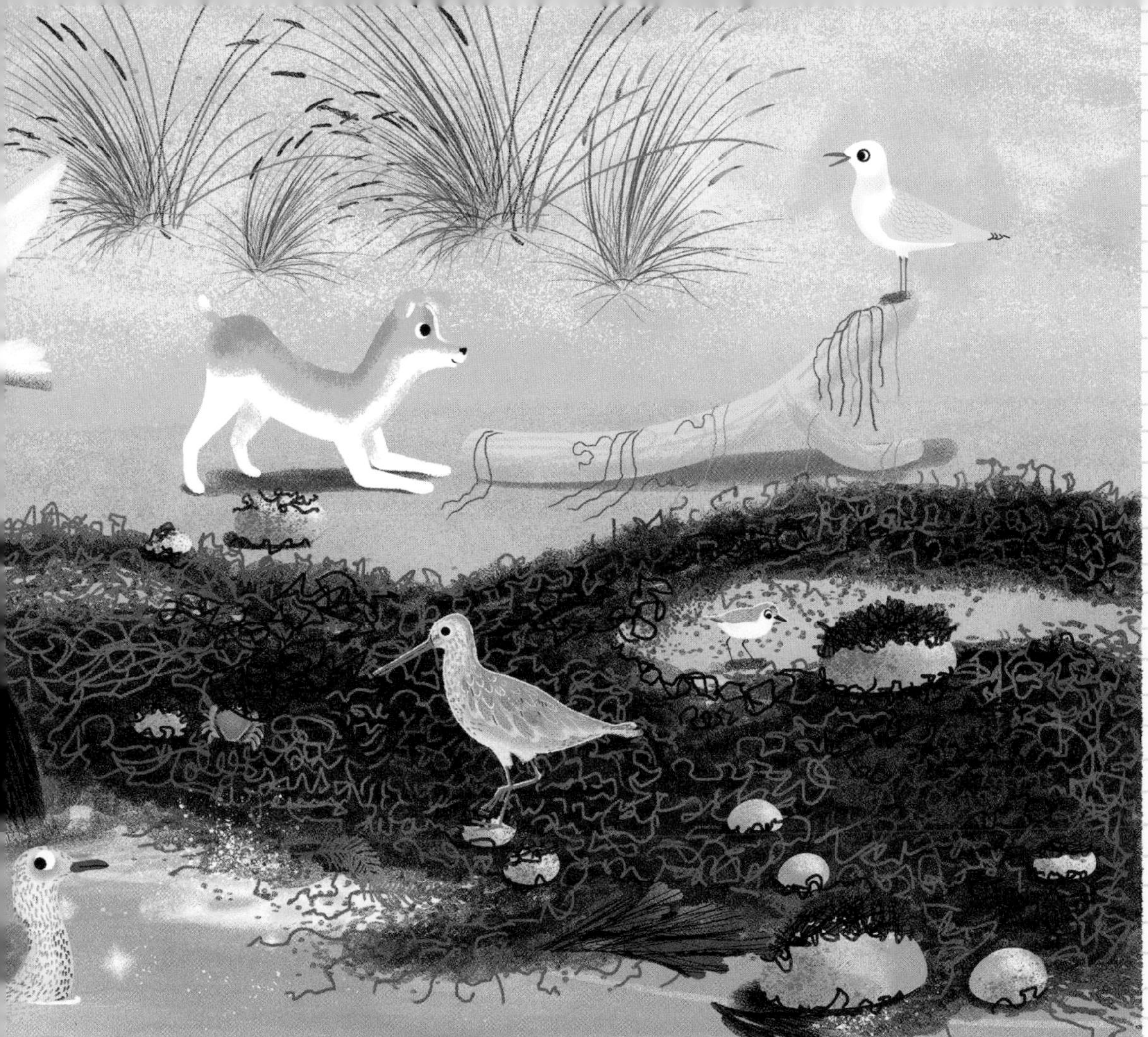

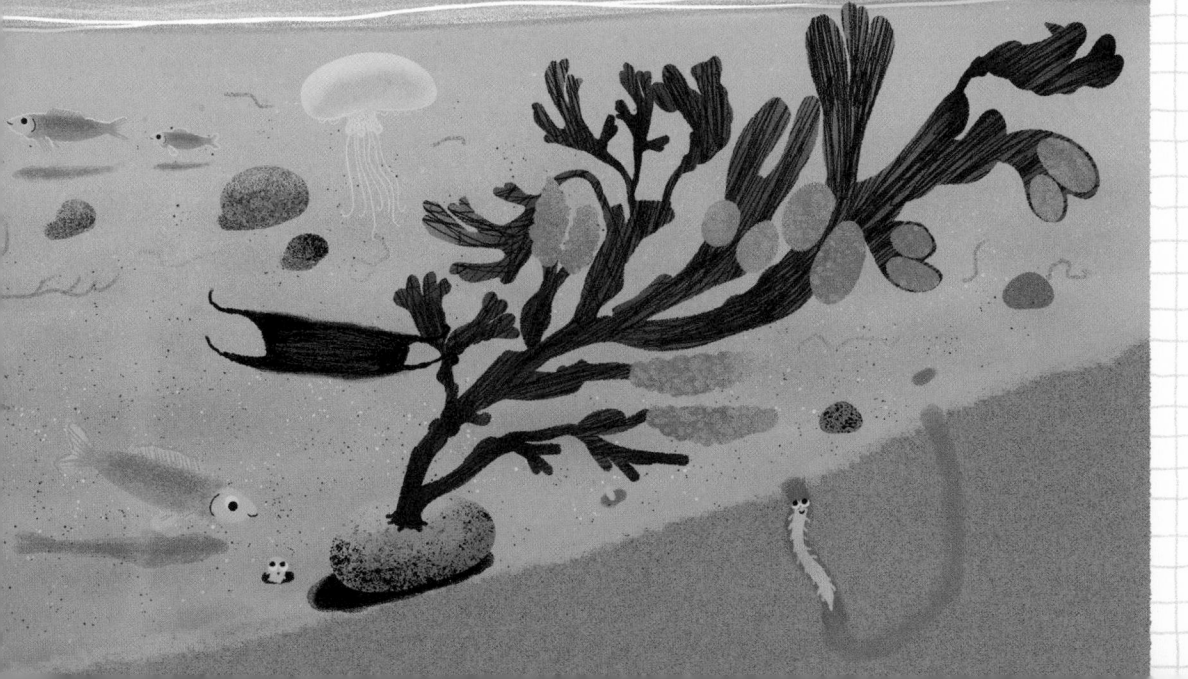

Mermaid’s purses are different shapes and sizes. You might even find a big one the size of a real money purse.

MERMAID’S PURSES TO SPOT:

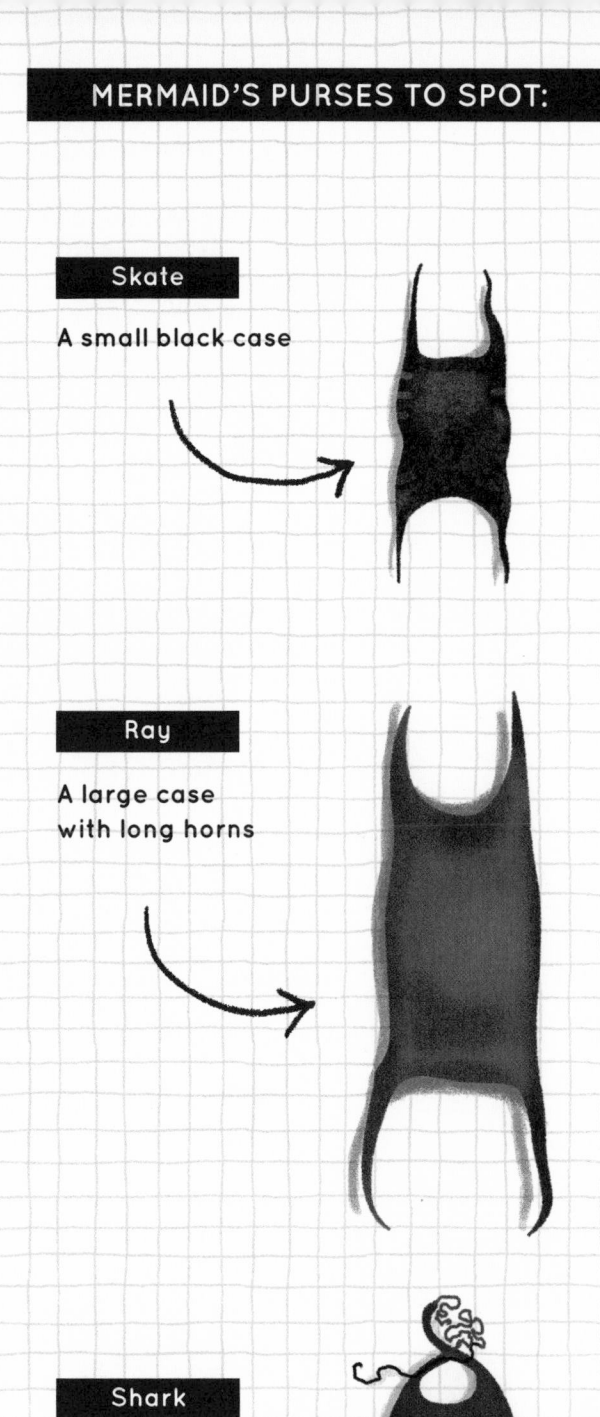

Skate

A small black case

Ray

A large case
with long horns

Shark

A case with
curly tendrils

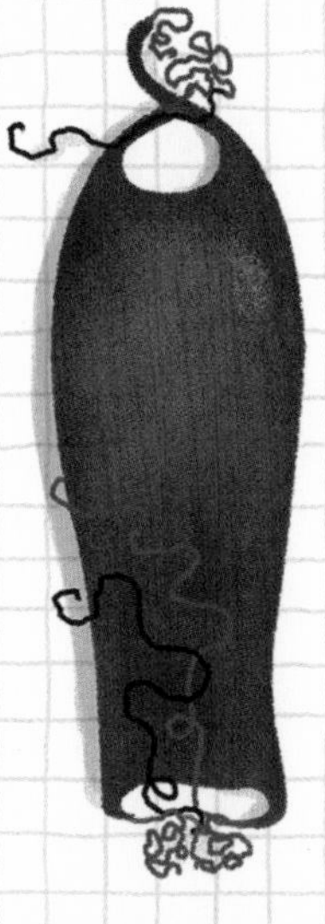

Up the cliff path. Follow me!
There's plenty more for us to see . . .

Look what I found!
A fossil of a sea urchin.
It looks like a picture of a star on a rock.

Can you also see . . . ?
One fluttery butterfly
Two bees busy buzzing around
Three different seaside flowers

Fossils are the bodies of animals or plants that died millions of years ago. The soft parts of the body disappear but the hard parts, such as shells, turn to rock.

Sometimes you might see the fossil of a plant stem or a leaf on a rock.

The star pattern on a sea urchin fossil is the top part of its shell.

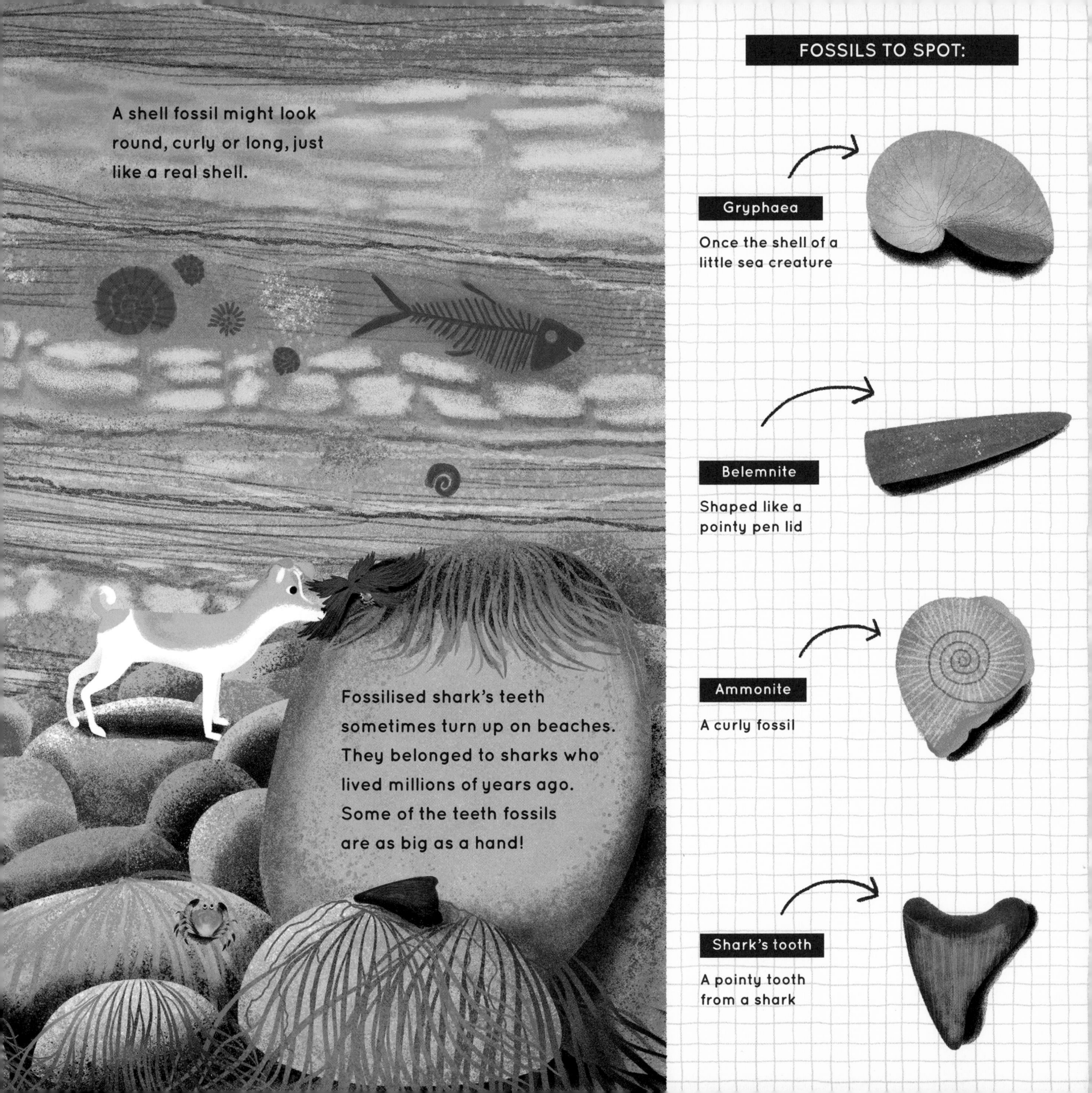

A shell fossil might look round, curly or long, just like a real shell.

Fossilised shark's teeth sometimes turn up on beaches. They belonged to sharks who lived millions of years ago. Some of the teeth fossils are as big as a hand!

FOSSILS TO SPOT:

Gryphaea

Once the shell of a little sea creature

Belemnite

Shaped like a pointy pen lid

Ammonite

A curly fossil

Shark's tooth

A pointy tooth from a shark

Gazing out across the bay
to ships and islands far away.

Look what I found!
A long feather, pointed like a pen.
Let's pretend to write in the air.

Can you also see . . . ?
One dog having fun
Two soaring seagulls
Three rabbits sitting in
the sunshine

Feathers keep birds warm
and dry like a waterproof coat.
They also help birds to fly.

Long feathers grow on
wings or tails. Short fluffy
feathers grow underneath.
They help to keep the bird
warm, like a cosy vest
under a jumper.

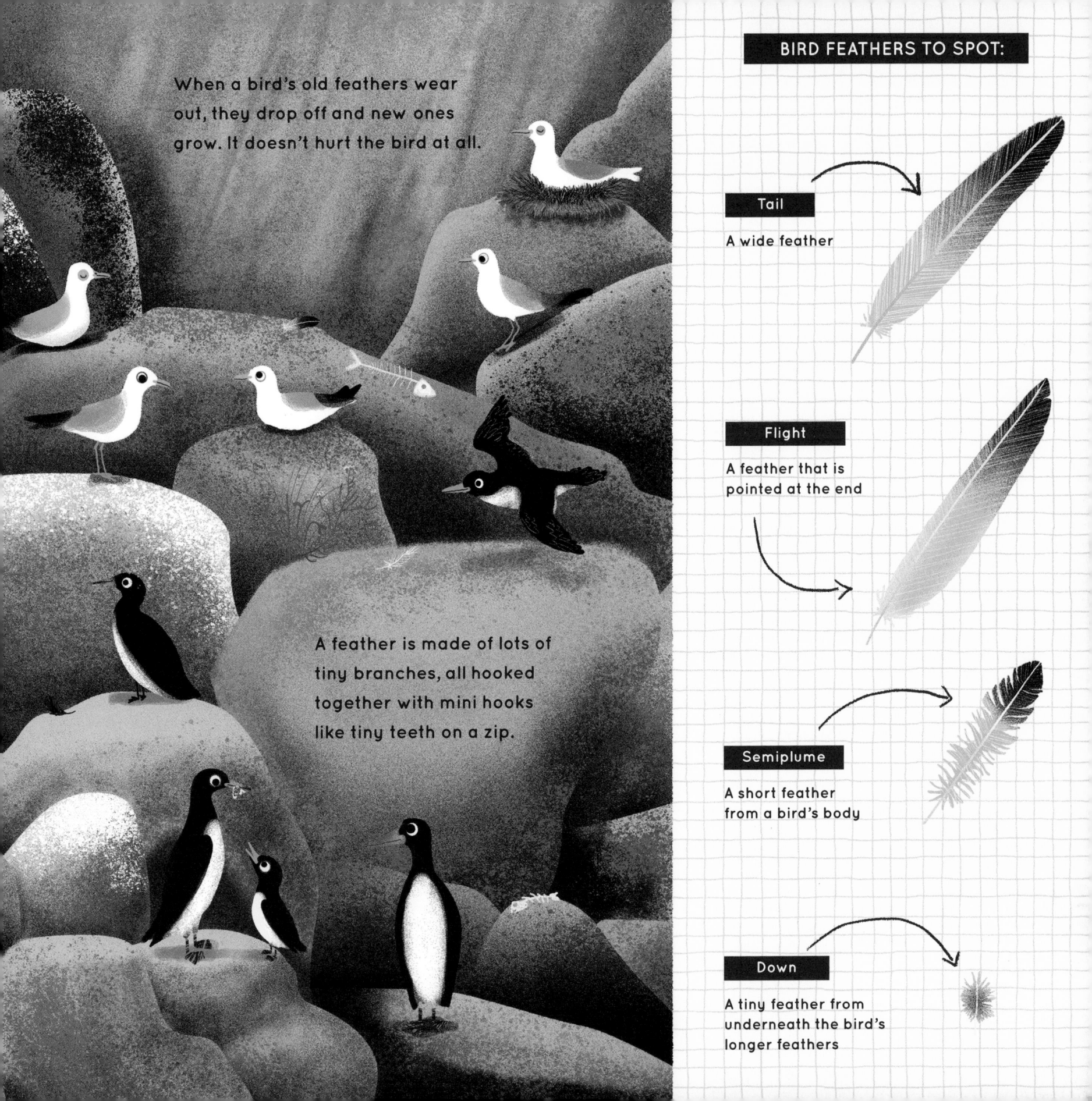

When a bird's old feathers wear out, they drop off and new ones grow. It doesn't hurt the bird at all.

A feather is made of lots of tiny branches, all hooked together with mini hooks like tiny teeth on a zip.

BIRD FEATHERS TO SPOT:

Tail

A wide feather

Flight

A feather that is pointed at the end

Semiplume

A short feather from a bird's body

Down

A tiny feather from underneath the bird's longer feathers

Goodbye beach.
We're homeward bound.

Look at all the things we've found . . .

...TREASURE!

As you collect, be thoughtful, too.
Bring no harm with what you do.

When you're exploring the seaside, make sure you help to look after it.
Never leave any litter behind you. Only collect a shell or two
and a couple of small pebbles.
Leave the rest so that the beach stays the way it should be.